I HAVE A
DREAM

DR. MARTIN LUTHER KING JR.

I HAVE A DREAM

Foreword by Amanda Gorman

MartinLuther King Jr. *Library*

Foreword Copyright © 2022 by Amanda Gorman

HarperCollins books may be purchased for educational, business, or
sales promotional use. For information, please email the Special Markets
Department at SPsales@harpercollins.com.

Designed by SBI Book Arts, LLC
Art © ARTvektor/Shutterstock

Library of Congress Cataloging-in-Publication Data
has been applied for.

ISBN 978-0-06-323679-0

22 23 24 25 26   LSC   10 9 8 7 6 5 4 3 2 1

Foreword

On January 20, 2021, I looked out at an almost-empty National Mall, preparing at the presidential inaugura-tion of Joe Biden. From my podium at the steps of the Capitol Building, I could see the tall, white glint of the Washington Monument obelisk, the early afternoon sun winking off the Lincoln Memorial Reflecting Pool, as well as the distant, massive marble work of the Lincoln Memorial itself. Seeing the striking silhou-ettes of these monuments gave my dangerously fluttering heart a physical piece of history to be grounded by. I forced my tight chest to take a deep breath and, looking out at the statues, let the first line of my poem "The Hill We Climb" leave my lips. Beat by beat, I put one word in front of another: "Mr. President, Madame Vice President, Americans, and the World."

As I spoke, I forced myself to wait and listen for the enormous ceremonial speakers to reverberate my words back to me before I continued to recite. This ensured that I wasn't talking over the long echoes of my own voice. It also let me privately embrace the echo of a moment of history from long before.

That moment was August 28, 1963, when Martin Luther King Jr. recited his now renowned speech "I Have a Dream" from the stairs of the Lincoln Memorial. Though Dr. King and I stood in different places and times when speaking, we were essentially looking out at the same reversed views: our country and its monuments.

Dr. King's speech would grow to become a monument in its own right, albeit one made of sentences and not stone. It touched not only the 250,000 people attending the March on Washington but also the countless others, born and unborn, who found a perennial power in his expressive cry for freedom and civil rights. Several attributes make it so powerful, including, but by no means limited to, three core elements: its vision, oratory, and language. That is: what it contains, how it was communicated, and the way it was composed.

First, Dr. King presented a unique revitalization of the American Dream that transcended race, class, gender, and other intersections of difference. In this way, it not only imagined a potent common ground but also chronicled the American conscience and condition.

The second strength of the speech lies in its extraordinary performance and execution. In the January days leading up to my recitation of "The Hill We Climb," I listened to recordings of the speech constantly, trying to learn from the reverend's electrifying and persuasive speaking style. Something we both share is the impact the Black church has had on our approach to public speaking. As a young Black girl who spent many a Sunday at my local Black church, my whole life I've been riveted by a long-standing institution that has produced Black prophets, poets, and change-makers through the ages, including the likes of Harriet Tubman and Frederick Douglass. In this, Dr. King is an extraordinary example, not an exclusive exception.

I'd also argue that Dr. King's speech endures not only because of its sturdy prose but also for its staggering poetry. Like the most wizened of rhapsodes, the ambitious reverend seamlessly marshals lyricism, figurative language, rhyme, rhythm, and rhetorical devices. His brilliant mastery of language enabled him to pen one of the most significant—and poetic—American texts in history.

Yet because his "I Have a Dream" speech remains so esteemed, some have argued that the text has become overused, cliché even. Granted, this speech is just one of the endless mediums through which Dr. King spoke out for justice. Nevertheless, the expansiveness of Dr. King's work doesn't preclude us from revisiting the indelible effect of "I Have a Dream." Reengaging thoroughly and curiously with such a work doesn't diminish Dr. King's lasting impact; rather, it deepens it. The more we open ourselves to the full breadth of his dream articulated, the more we open ourselves to the full breadth of our shared future. That is to say, even what is renowned must be re-known, again and again, if it is to have any lasting meaning.

It would've been impossible for me to write "The Hill We Climb" without approaching "I Have a Dream" as one of the poem's many literary ancestors. If anything, it reminded me that although I stood separate and apart at the inaugural podium, I was far from alone. I was participating in a long heritage of public figures who find unfading inspiration from Dr. King's activism. We revisit "I Have a Dream" not to become Dr. King but to further behold, bear up, and bring forth the entirety of his life's work. He was a singular meteor whose trajectory no one can copy, but his mission is one we can continue. That is the everlasting and *ever-growing* power of Dr. King's dream. It is a hope that challenges, demands, and welcomes us all.

The instant I finished reciting "The Hill We Climb," I could hear the slow but sure sound of the speakers blaring back at me in the crisp winter air. It was as if history itself were speaking back, reminding me of all the other giants, all the other Kings, whose shoulders I am fortunate enough to stand on. My poem may have been a solo performance, but I was just one voice in a chorus of people who continue to call back to Dr. King's surviving vision. I smiled, truly believing, as I still do, that the echo of Dr. King's work will always reverberate loud and clear. What's more, one day it won't be just an echo but an existence—not just a dream fiercely ringing but a dream finally realized.

—Amanda Gorman

Los Angeles, CA

2022

"I HAVE A DREAM" SPEECH

August 28, 1963

I am happy to join
with you today in what will
go down in history as the
greatest demonstration
for freedom in the
history of our nation.

Five score years ago,

a great American,

in whose symbolic shadow

we stand today, signed

the Emancipation

Proclamation.

This momentous decree
came as a great beacon light
of hope to millions of
Negro slaves who had
been seared in the flames
of withering injustice.

It came as a joyous

daybreak to end the long

night of their captivity.

But one hundred years later,

the Negro still is not free.

One hundred years later,

the life of the Negro is still

sadly crippled by the manacles

of segregation and the

chains of discrimination.

One hundred years later,
the Negro lives on a lonely
island of poverty in the
midst of a vast ocean of
material prosperity.

One hundred years later,
the Negro is still languished
in the corners of American
society and finds himself
in exile in his own land.

And so we've come here

today to dramatize a

shameful condition.

In a sense we've come

to our nation's capital

to cash a check.

When the architects of
our republic wrote the
magnificent words
of the Constitution and
the Declaration of
Independence, they were
signing a promissory note
to which every American
was to fall heir.

This note was a promise that
all men, yes, black men as
well as white men, would be
guaranteed the unalienable
rights of life, liberty, and
the pursuit of happiness.

It is obvious today that America has defaulted on this promissory note insofar as her citizens of color are concerned.

Instead of honoring this sacred obligation, America has given the Negro people a bad check, a check which has come back marked insufficient funds.

But we refuse to believe

that the bank of justice

is bankrupt.

We refuse to believe that

there are insufficient

funds in the great vaults of

opportunity of this nation.

And so we've come to

cash this check,

a check that will give us

upon demand the

riches of freedom

and the security

of justice.

We have also come to
this hallowed spot to
remind America of the
fierce urgency of now.

This is no time to engage

in the luxury of cooling off

or to take the tranquilizing

drug of gradualism.

Now is the time to
make real the promises
of democracy.

Now is the time to

rise from the dark and

desolate valley of segregation

to the sunlit path of

racial justice.

Now is the time

to lift our nation from

the quicksands of racial

injustice to the solid

rock of brotherhood.

Now is the time
to make justice a reality
for all of God's children.

It would be fatal for the

nation to overlook the

urgency of the moment.

This sweltering summer of
the Negro's legitimate
discontent will not pass until
there is an invigorating autumn
of freedom and equality.

1963 is not an end,

but a beginning.

And those who hope that the Negro needed to blow off steam and will now be content will have a rude awakening if the nation returns to business as usual.

There will be neither rest
nor tranquility in America
until the Negro is granted
his citizenship rights.

The whirlwinds of revolt

will continue to shake

the foundations of our

nation until the bright

day of justice emerges.

But there is something that
I must say to my people,
who stand on the warm
threshold which leads into
the palace of justice:

in the process of gaining

our rightful place,

we must not be guilty of

wrongful deeds.

Let us not seek to satisfy

our thirst for freedom by

drinking from the cup of

bitterness and hatred.

We must forever conduct our struggle on the high plane of dignity and discipline. We must not allow our creative protest to degenerate into physical violence.

Again and again,
we must rise to the majestic
heights of meeting physical
force with soul force.

The marvelous new militancy

which has engulfed the

Negro community must

not lead us to a distrust

of all white people,

for many of our white

brothers, as evidenced by

their presence here today,

have come to realize that
their destiny is tied up with
our destiny, and they have
come to realize that their
freedom is inextricably
bound to our freedom.

We cannot walk alone.

And as we walk, we must
make the pledge that we
shall always march ahead.
We cannot turn back.

There are those who are asking

the devotees of civil rights,

"When will you be satisfied?"

We can never be satisfied as long as the Negro is the victim of the unspeakable horrors of police brutality.

We can never be satisfied

as long as our bodies, heavy

with the fatigue of travel,

cannot gain lodging in the

motels of the highways and

the hotels of the cities.

We cannot be satisfied as long as the Negro's basic mobility is from a smaller ghetto to a larger one.

We can never be satisfied

as long as our children are

stripped of their selfhood and

robbed of their dignity by

signs stating for whites only.

We cannot be satisfied as long as a Negro in Mississippi cannot vote and a Negro in New York believes he has nothing for which to vote.

No, no, we are not satisfied

and we will not be satisfied

until justice rolls down like

waters and righteousness

like a mighty stream.

I am not unmindful that some
of you have come here out of
great trials and tribulations.

Some of you have come fresh

from narrow jail cells.

Some of you have come from areas where your quest for freedom left you battered by the storms of persecution and staggered by the winds of police brutality. You have been the veterans of creative suffering.

Continue to work with
the faith that unearned
suffering is redemptive.

Go back to Mississippi,

go back to Alabama,

go back to South Carolina,

go back to Georgia,

go back to Louisiana,

go back to the slums

and ghettos of our

northern cities,

knowing that somehow

this situation can and

will be changed.

Let us not wallow in
the valley of despair.

I say to you today, my friends,

so even though we face

the difficulties of today

and tomorrow,

I still have a dream.

It is a dream deeply rooted

in the American dream.

I have a dream that one day this nation will rise up and live out the true meaning of its creed: "We hold these truths to be self-evident, that all men are created equal."

I have a dream that one day
on the red hills of Georgia, the
sons of former slaves and the
sons of former slave owners will
be able to sit down together
at the table of brotherhood.

I have a dream that one day
even the state of Mississippi,
a state sweltering with
the heat of injustice,

sweltering with the

heat of oppression,

will be transformed into

an oasis of freedom

and justice.

I have a dream that my four little children will one day live in a nation where they will not be judged by the color of their skin but by the content of their character.

I have a dream today.

I have a dream that one day

down in Alabama, with

its vicious racists,

with its governor having

his lips dripping with the

words of "interposition"

and "nullification,"

one day right there in Alabama

little black boys and black girls

will be able to join hands with

little white boys and white

girls as sisters and brothers.

I have a dream today.

I have a dream that one day

every valley shall be exalted,

every hill and mountain

shall be made low,

the rough places will be made

plain, and the crooked places

will be made straight,

and the glory of the Lord

shall be revealed, and all

flesh shall see it together.

This is our hope.

This is the faith that I go
back to the South with.

With this faith we will be able

to hew out of the mountain

of despair a stone of hope.

With this faith we will be
able to transform the
jangling discords of our
nation into a beautiful
symphony of brotherhood.

With this faith we will be

able to work together,

to pray together,

to struggle together,

to go to jail together,

to stand up for

freedom together,

knowing that we will

be free one day.

This will be the day,

this will be the day when all

of God's children will be able

to sing with new meaning:

"My country, 'tis of thee,

sweet land of liberty,

of thee I sing.

Land where my fathers died,

land of the pilgrim's pride,

from every mountainside,

let freedom ring!"

And if America is to be a great

nation, this must become true.

So let freedom ring

from the prodigious hilltops

of New Hampshire.

Let freedom ring

from the mighty mountains

of New York.

Let freedom ring

from the heightening

Alleghenies of Pennsylvania.

Let freedom ring

from the snow-capped

Rockies of Colorado.

Let freedom ring
from the curvaceous
slopes of California.

But not only that:

Let freedom ring

from Stone Mountain

of Georgia.

Let freedom ring

from Lookout Mountain

of Tennessee.

Let freedom ring

from every hill and

molehill of Mississippi.

From every mountainside,

let freedom ring.

And when this happens,

and when we allow

freedom to ring,

when we let it ring from

every village and every hamlet,

from every state and every city,

we will be able to speed up

that day when all of

God's children,

black men and white

men, Jews and Gentiles,

Protestants and Catholics,

will be able to join hands

and sing in the words of

the old Negro spiritual:

"Free at last! Free at last!

Thank God Almighty,

we are free at last!"

Resources

"I Have a Dream" is just the beginning of understanding
King's profound impact on America and the world.
The following list represents just a portion of the many
resources available on King and on "I Have a Dream."

FILMOGRAPHY

All the Way (2016). This film is about events during the
presidency of Lyndon Baines Johnson and his relationship
with Martin Luther King Jr. It was originally a Broadway
play of the same name.

Boycott (2001). A film based on the book *Daybreak of Freedom:
The Montgomery Bus Boycott*, edited by Stewart Burns (Chapel
Hill: Univ. of North Carolina Press, 1997).

Bringing King to China (2011). A documentary film about a young American woman attempting to bring King's belief in nonviolence to China.

Eyes on the Prize I and *II* (1987 and 1990). The definitive, award-winning, fourteen-episode PBS documentary series (six episodes in part I, 1987; eight episodes in part II, 1990) about the Black Freedom Struggle (also known as the Civil Rights Movement) in the United States and Martin Luther King's role in it. The series features interviews with participants, historical perspective, and narration by Julian Bond.

King (1978). A television miniseries based on the life of Martin Luther King Jr., featuring luminary actors Ossie Davis, Cicely Tyson, Paul Winfield, and Roscoe Lee Browne.

King: A Filmed Record . . . Montgomery to Memphis (1970). A documentary film biography of King and his leadership of the Black Freedom Struggle using only original newsreels and other primary materials. An excellent source of unretouched news footage on the Black Freedom Struggle, featuring celebrity narrations by Ruby Dee, Charlton Heston, James Earl Jones, Burt Lancaster, Paul Newman, and Joanne Woodward.

MLK/FBI (2020). A documentary film by Sam Pollard (co-director of *Eyes on the Prize*) that follows King's harassment by J. Edgar Hoover and the Federal Bureau of Investigation.

Our Friend, Martin (1999). A children's education film about King and the Black Freedom Struggle. The film follows two middle school friends who travel back in time, meeting King at various points during his life.

Path to War (2002). Although principally about the Vietnam War as seen through the eyes of US president Lyndon Baines Johnson, King's opposition to the war is included through the character portraying him. King's opposition to the Vietnam War was mentioned most prominently in his 1967 "Beyond Vietnam" speech at Riverside Church in New York City.

Rustin (2022). A Netflix film about Bayard Rustin, who planned the March on Washington in 1963. The film, produced by Barack Obama's company Higher Ground Productions, re-creates the events leading up to the march and King's historic "I Have a Dream" speech.

Selma (2014). A historical drama based on the 1965 Selma to Montgomery voting rights march, featuring the song "Glory" (music and lyrics by John Legend and Common), which won the 2014 Best Original Song Oscar.

Selma, Lord, Selma (1999). A biographical drama based on the events, known as Blood Sunday, that happened in Selma at the time of the Selma to Montgomery march in March 1965.

The film examines those events through the eyes of a Sheyann Webb, also known as King's "Smallest Freedom Fighter," who co-authored the book *Selma, Lord, Selma* (Tuscaloosa: Univ. of Alabama Press, 1997).

We Are the Dream: The Kids of the Oakland MLK Oratorical Fest (2020). An HBO documentary film about the youth who participate in an annual public speaking competition honoring the legacy of Martin Luther King Jr.

DISCOGRAPHY

There are many recordings of King speaking and preaching at various venues. Of these, the following stand out in their relationship to his delivery of "I Have a Dream" at the March on Washington.

Funeral Services: Ebenezer Baptist Church, April 9, 1968 (1968, LP, Brotherhood Records). This tribute to King after his assassination includes a recording of his delivery of "I Have a Dream" at the March on Washington.

Ils on marché sur la terre (*They Walked the Earth*; 1999, CDs, Rsr). This three-CD compilation features King talking about "I Have a Dream" along with interviews of Desmond Tutu, His Holiness the Dalai Lama, Elie Wiesel, and others.

We Shall Overcome (1963, LP, Council for United Civil Rights Leadership). The definitive recording of the March on Washington, featuring King delivering the "I Have a Dream" speech along with other speeches and songs by Odetta, Bob Dylan, Joan Baez, Marian Anderson, and Peter, Paul, and Mary.

BIBLIOGRAPHY (Adult)

With so many books written about the life and legacy of Martin Luther King Jr., the following five were selected for their relevancy to the March on Washington and the "I Have a Dream" speech.

The Autobiography of Martin Luther King, Jr., edited by Clayborne Carson (New York: Warner Books, 1998). Carson was selected by Coretta Scott King, King's widow, to edit and publish her late husband's papers. Carson was, for more than thirty years, the head of the Martin Luther King Jr. archives at Stanford University. This book features original source material and Carson's keen insight into King's major speeches, including "I Have a Dream."

Martin Luther King, Jr.: A Life, by Marshall Frady (New York: Penguin, 2002). Marshall Frady was an award-winning reporter who worked for *Newsweek*, *Life*, *Harper's*, *Esquire*, *The*

New York Review of Books, The Sunday Times of the UK, *The New Yorker,* and ABC News. His reporting focused principally on the Black Southern Freedom Movement during the 1960s. This is a relatively short biography of King that features Frady's observations on the "I Have a Dream" speech and the March on Washington.

Martin Luther King: The Inconvenient Hero, by Vincent Harding (Maryknoll, NY: Orbis Books, 2013). Vincent Harding was King's friend, confidant, and speechwriter. Harding wrote the "Beyond Vietnam" speech, which many believed marked King for death. Harding delves deeply into the "I Have a Dream" speech, and why it has become the principal memory for King as a "convenient hero" in the eyes of most Americans, when King's legacy is so much greater than "I Have a Dream."

Parting the Waters: America in the King Years, 1954–63, by Taylor Branch (New York: Simon & Schuster, 1988). Author Taylor Branch won a Pulitzer Prize for this in-depth examination of the Freedom Struggle in America, leading up to the March on Washington. It is important context for understanding what came before that pivotal moment on the steps of the Lincoln Memorial.

What Manner of Man: A Biography of Martin Luther King, Jr., by Lerone Bennett Jr. (Chicago: Johnson Publishing, 2000). Bennett was the senior editor of *Ebony* and a preeminent scholar of African American history. His insights into "I Have a Dream" and King's legacy are essential to a full understanding of the man.

BIBLIOGRAPHY (Children)

Preschool

A Sweet Smell of Roses, by Angela Johnson (author) and Eric Velasquez (illustrator) (New York: Simon & Schuster, 2007). This book, by three-time Coretta Scott King Award–winning author Angela Johnson, portrays the young children involved in the March on Washington and the Black Freedom Struggle in America.

I Am Martin Luther King, Jr. (Ordinary People Change the World series), by Brad Meltzer (author) and Christopher Eliopoulos (illustrator) (New York: Dial Books, 2016). A *New York Times* bestselling picture book that introduces King to young children as the hero they, too, can be.

Elementary School

A Place to Land: Martin Luther King Jr. and the Speech That Inspired a Nation, by Barry Wittenstein (author) and Jerry Pinkney (illustrator) (New York: Neal Porter Books, 2019).

A riveting, inspirational story about King's "I Have a Dream" speech for younger readers, illustrated by legendary author and illustrator Jerry Pinkney.

I Have a Dream, by Martin Luther King Jr. (New York: Schwartz & Wade Books, 2012). With illustrations by Caldecott Medal–winning illustrator Kabir Nelson, the book and CD present a powerful way for children to first come to apprehend the meaning and importance of King's speech at the March on Washington.

Middle School

Martin Rising: Requiem for a King, by Andrea Davis Pinkney (author) and Brian Pinkney (illustrator) (New York: Scholastic Press, 2018). Award-winning illustrator Brian Pinkney brings to life the simple yet lyrical poetry of award-winning author Andrea Davis Pinkney.

Who Was Martin Luther King, Jr.?, by Bonnie Bader (author) and Elizabeth Wolf (illustrator) (New York: Penguin, 2007). From the Montgomery bus boycott through the March on Washington, and beyond, this book for young readers explains a tumultuous time in the US through clear text and eighty compelling black-and-white illustrations.

Dear Martin, by Nic Stone (New York: Crown, 2017). After a traffic stop turns violent, Justyce, a young man, writes a journal to Martin Luther King Jr., reflecting on King's dream and what it means for Justyce's future in this #1 *New York Times* bestseller.

TEACHING RESOURCES

"The Best of Our Dr. Martin Luther King Jr. Resources." Lessons plans, podcast, and a host of resources about King, "I Have a Dream," and the Black Freedom Struggle in America, from Learning for Justice, at https://www.learning forjustice.org/magazine/the-best-of-our-dr-martin-luther -king-jr-resources.

"Classroom Resources for Martin Luther King Jr. Day." See the extensive set of resources and curriculum guides from the National Education Association, at https://www.nea.org /professional-excellence/student-engagement/tools-tips/class room-resources-martin-luther-king-jr-day.

"King Resources." From Stanford University's Martin Luther King, Jr. Research and Education Institute. Thousands of documents, photographs, and publications, at https://king

institute.stanford.edu/king-resources/king-resources
-overview.

Martin Luther King Jr. Lessons, Worksheets, and Activities.
Classroom materials for educators from Teacher Planet,
at https://www.teacherplanet.com/content/martin-luther
-king-jr.

"Teaching King Beyond 'I Have a Dream.'" Lesson plans
and resources from the Teaching for Change organization,
at https://www.civilrightsteaching.org/teaching-martin
-luther-king-jr.

About Dr. Martin Luther King Jr.

Dr. Martin Luther King Jr. (1929–1968), civil rights leader and recipient of the Nobel Prize for Peace, inspired and sustained the struggle for freedom, nonviolence, interracial brotherhood, and social justice.

About Amanda Gorman

Amanda Gorman is the youngest presidential inaugural poet in US history. She is a committed advocate for the environment, racial equality, and gender justice. After graduating cum laude from Harvard University, she now lives in her hometown of Los Angeles. Amanda was one of five *Variety* Power of Women honorees and cover star, one of three cover stars for *Glamour*'s Women of the Year, and one of *TIME* magazine's Women of the Year. The special edition of her inaugural poem, "The Hill We Climb," was published in March 2021. Her debut picture book, *Change Sings*, was released in September 2021, and her poetry collection, *Call Us What We Carry*, was released in December 2021, all debuting at number one on the *New York Times*, *USA Today*, and *Wall Street Journal* bestsellers lists. Please visit theamandagorman.com.